William Davies

The Shepherd's Garden

William Davies

The Shepherd's Garden

ISBN/EAN: 9783337074999

Printed in Europe, USA, Canada, Australia, Japan

Cover: Foto ©ninafisch / pixelio.de

More available books at **www.hansebooks.com**

THE SHEPHERD'S GARDEN.

BY

WILLIAM DAVIES,

AUTHOR OF 'SONGS OF A WAYFARER,' ETC.

LONDON:
SAMPSON LOW, MARSTON, LOW AND SEARLE,
CROWN BUILDINGS, 188, FLEET STREET.
1873.

[All rights reserved.]

LONDON:
PRINTED BY W. CLOWES AND SONS, STAMFORD STREET
AND CHARING CROSS.

L OUERS when they come into a Gardeine, some gather Nettles, some Roses, one Tyme, an other Sage, and euerye one that for his Ladyes fauour that she fauoreth: insomuch as there is no Weede almost but it is worne. If you, Gentlemen, doe the lyke in reading, I shall bee sure all my discourses shall be regarded, some for the smell, some for the smart, all for a kinde of a louing smacke. Lette euerye one followe his fancie, and say that is best which he lyketh best. And so I commit euerye mans delight to his own choice and my selfe to all your courtesies.

JOHN LYLY. *Euphues.* 1580.

CONTENTS.

	PAGE
INDUCTION	1
COUNTRY PLEASURES	6
THE TEMPEST	7
THE SHEPHERD BOY'S SONG	8
SPRING-TIME	10
THE DANCE	11
SONG. 'LEAD ME WELCOME PLEASURE'	12
THE MAY QUEEN	13
PHILLIS AND COLIN	14
MAY MORNING	15
LOVE A SERGEANT	16
THE AWAKENING OF DAPHNE	18
THE SWEET SEASON	19
TO PAN	20
A MADRIGAL. 'IN FAIR ARCADIA IT FELL'	25
ALEXIS' RESOLVE	26
COUNTRY CONTENTMENTS	27

	PAGE
THE SHEPHERD TO HIS MISTRESS	29
DIANA AND ENDYMION	31
A MADRIGAL. 'ON A FAIR DAY'	33
THE SHEPHERD'S WOOING	34
THE QUARREL	35
AN INVITATION TO BANISH SADNESS	36
THE PENSIVE SHEPHERD	38
THE SHEPHERD'S HOLIDAY	40
THE FESTIVAL	41
THE LITTLE BIRD'S SONG	42
TO A SINGING THRUSH	43
THE SHEPHERD INVOKES THE WOODLAND BIRD TO TELL HIM OF HIS MISTRESS	47
THE SHEPHERD PRAYS HIS MISTRESS TO SPEAK HER AFFECTION	48
LOVE'S ALCHEMY	49
CUPID'S THEFT	50
THE SHEPHERD'S SCORN OF LOVE	51
THE FERRY	52
MAGNUS DEUS SAPPHO	53
HERO	54
JOVE'S CHEAT	55
THE IDEAL	57
CANZONET. 'KISS ME, FAIR LOVE'	58
CAST AWAY CARE!	59
LOVE WILL FIND A WAY	60
STOP THIEF!	62

CONTENTS.

	PAGE
Love's Deceit	63
The Interdiction	64
The Vow	65
The Shepherd to his Mistress with a Lute	66
The Force of Music	67
The Inconstant	68
The Shepherd complains to his Mistress when she will forego their Love	71
The Tryst	73
The Lost Bird	74
A Complaint of the Falsity of Time	76
Love's Funeral	77
Lips and Roses	79
Corydon's Lament	80
Funeral Song	82
Forewarning	84
Love's Stratagem	87
Counsel to the Lover of a Light Mistress	88
Love's Repaying	91
Cupid's Treachery	92
All things to my Love am I	93
The Shepherd ridicules the false Charms of a Flaunting Beauty	95
Wooing and Wedding	97
The Strife	99
Ceres' Triumph	102
The Song of the Plough	103

CONTENTS.

	PAGE
The Death of Summer	106
Winter	107
The Yule-tide Message	109
Welcome to Christmas	111
A Christmas Carol	114
The Shepherd renounces his Youthful Fancies	115
Mutability	117
The Epitome	119
The Shepherd will follow his best Mistress, Virtue, wherever she may lead him	120
The Shepherd under the figure of a fair Mistress praises Divine Philosophy	121
The Love of the Highest	130
Retirement	132
The Rest	139
Shepherd's Thrift	142
The Shepherd's Good Night	145

THE SHEPHERD'S GARDEN.

INDUCTION.

APOLLO raised aloft his golden head,
    Crowning each peak and purple shining spire;
The upward lark above the misty mead
    Began to warble forth his new desire:
The shepherd drove his woolly flocks to feed
    Along the mountain-side; in quaint attire
The milking-maid tript forth, and so did sing,
All nature seemed to join her carolling.

Along the hedgerows drooping buds were seen
    To lift themselves and shake the dew-drops bright:
The trees revived, and through their robes of green,
    Rustled their airy leaves for much delight;
The blissful wind slid o'er the plain to glean
    The vapoury fragments of the parting night:
The laughing brooks leapt merrily along,
And cheered their flowery way with many a song.

The labourer shouted in the furrowed field;
　The bark of dogs from upland farms was blown;
Whilst cawing rooks about the elm-trees wheel'd
　That high above the gabled grange had grown;
And all the vale a sense of peace did yield
　From quiet homestead and from hamlet brown:
The newly-baptized world to heaven looked up,
And smiled in gladness of fresh springing hope.

Then did I waken from my sleepy bed,
　And gat me from my couch right joyfully;
And by a crystal streamlet lightly led,
　I spied a shepherd swain reclined thereby;
A leafy garland set upon his head,
　And by his side a pipe of reed did lie;
And thus he sang, whilst all the solitude
With echoing voice his happy strain renew'd:—

O world of false delights, why do you make
　This pleasant garden such a den of care;
And all these rural joys do scorn to take,
　Whose tender hours with rest so woven are?
Why will you seek for pain, and peace forsake,
　Nor ever to these pleasant bowers repair?
Why is your love set on such worthless things,
When Nature makes you these fair offerings?

Your wealth can buy no carpet like these leas;
　　No costliest scents these blossoms can surpass,
Whose tinctured lips breathe perfume on the breeze:
　　Your brightest mirrors dull beside the glass
Of these clear pools; your proudest palaces,
　　Through which the painted shows of beauty pass,
Match not these shady woods whose twilight halls
Are filled with sound of winds and waterfalls.

Are we athirst; pure wells our thirst can slake:
　　Would we be fanned; cool breezes pass us by:
If we desire repose, soft turf doth make
　　Our couch, with birds to sing our lullaby:
The winding stream, broad pastures, wood and brake,
　　More fair than pictures to our gazing lie:
All things in heaven and under heaven combined,
Do make the empire of a quiet mind.

So wealthy are the souls that live at ease,
　　Whom sweet content with gold and lands doth bless,
And wholesome Nature's simplest charms do please
　　With more than worth of worldly happiness:
For them the brook doth flow, and spreading trees
　　Their welcome shade of murmuring leaves do dress,
And Joy doth wait in byeways them to meet,
Their fixed serenities with smiles to greet.—

Thus as he sang the shining sun did mount
    His azure throne, and all the woods were still;
Only the silvery lapping of the fount
    Was heard within the shadow of the hill:
From hour to hour the westering day did count
    His tranquil thinkings, and the air did fill
His heart with joy, wherefrom this happy verse
Distilled like incense through the universe.

Then as the gilded hours did glide away,
    He sang these songs which now I write for you,
Whilst from a neighbouring thicket all the day,
    A throstle whistled, and a far cuckoo,
Kissing the sleeping Silence where it lay
    Until it woke and faintly sang thereto,
Called through the afternoon the fairest night
That ever stars with beams of love made bright:

Then rose, and taking up his pipe, began
    To pipe thereon his master melodies:
With nimble fingers up and down he ran,
    That Pan his own best cunning might despise,
And stay his vanquished breath with envy wan,
    Feeding his ear with such felicities
As breed within their tones forlorn despairs,
For that no stop of his can touch such airs.

Each tuneful note sang like a summer linnet
   Whose heart the generous season doth unbind,
When thronèd Love sits jubilant within it,
   O'erjoyed such fitting domicile to find,
As though from earth to heaven it would win it.
   Adieu! he cried, ye fields: may Heaven be kind
To banish from your borders every sorrow,
And morning wake you to as fair a morrow.

COUNTRY PLEASURES.

COME, and I will take you
    Where the lambs are playing,
And of our band will make you—
    Young lads and lasses maying.
Hark! do you hear the field-boy's horn a-blowing,
And all the cows about the meadows lowing,
    And round the woodland cheerful noise
Of merry birds that make the heart rejoice?
    Here is such store
Of painted flowers that gardens have no more:
    As daffodils
    That fringe the rills,
Millions of daisies sparkling on the floor,
With pink anemones and mayflowers,
Talking to one another in the bowers;
    Bright fountains falling down,
    By soft winds overblown:
All bidding care and sorrow go away
    On this so fair a day.
Such sweet delights this rural life can give,
None would desire in busy towns to live.

THE TEMPEST.

BRIGHT PHŒBUS doth his light assuage
   Behind a watery cloud;
The angry waves begin to rage
   And Jove to thunder loud;
The ash doth bend, the oak doth crack,
   The lightning flashes bright between;
Whilst robed in billowy folds of black,
   The frowning heavens are seen.
But now there comes a little ray
   Doth herald in the brighter day;
And hark! the birds begin to sing,
Forewarning harbingers of spring:
Lo, the soft south comes back again
With odoured airs across the plain,
And the sweet morning kisses rise
To glad the light in Beauty's eyes.

THE SHEPHERD-BOY'S SONG.

TRA la ro!
    Mildly blow,
Wind of morn: thou little lamb,
Skip and frisk it near thy dam:
Bird, be blithe upon the bough:
Whistle, ploughman at the plough:
Shout, brave shepherd: oxen, low!
    Tra la ro!

Tra la ro!
    Streamlet, flow:
Mill go round, and miller laugh:
Bee to flower, honey quaff:
Calf, be thou right glad to-day:
Hedge, grow white with scented may:
Grass, be greener: blossom, blow!
    Tra la ro!

Tra la ro!
    Cheerily ho!
Mirth be met of man and boy:
Frolic child pour out thy joy!

Sky, let all thy sunshine loose!
Lisping lovers, come and choose:
Hark, the herdsman's horn doth blow,
    Tra la ro!

    Tra la ro!
    Sadness go!
Shepherd, pipe it merrily;
Pipe, nor let dull echo die;
Pipe in valley, pipe on hill;
Pipe from morn to night thy fill;
Pipe and sing both high and low,
    Tra la ro!

SPRING-TIME.

NOW doth the sun shine cheerily,
And lambs are skipping merrily.
    Fa la la.

Sweet maids, put on your kirtles,
And deck your hair with myrtles.
    Fa la la.

Earth pranks her verdant bosom
With many an opening blossom.
    Fa la la.

Come let us tread a measure,
And seize the spring-time pleasure.
    Fa la la.

THE DANCE.

DINDERLY, danderly, merrily seen,
  Gay lads and lasses dance over the green;
With mirth and with play we drive care away,
Triumphantly banished this bright holiday.
These shady old trees our fancies do please,
As we trip it and slip it and skip it along.
    This is my song:
    Trip it along!

Fairily, airily, see how we go,
Faithfully footing it all in a row!
The woodland around re-echoes the sound
Of tabor and fife in a gladsome rebound.
All hearts are alive, sweet pleasures revive,
As we trip it and slip it and skip it along.
    Sing to my song:
    Slip it along!

Warily, Margery: go not so fast:
Overhaste at the parting shall not be to last.
Sweet Bessie, beware, or the gins of thy hair
The heart of bold Reuben with love may ensnare.
Hark! the glad strain now recalls us again
To trip it and slip it and skip it along,
    Singing this song:
    Skip it along!

SONG.

LEAD me, welcome Pleasure,
    Queen and sister bright,
Where airy footsteps measure
    Pied pastures of delight!
Our jolly pastime sharing
Brave Beauty beams unsparing.

Sit we now reposing
    Down in the flowery glade,
White flocks about us dozing;
    The shepherd in the shade.
Calm rest from toil inviteth :
The hour in peace delighteth.

THE SHEPHERD'S GARDEN.

THE MAY QUEEN.

LOVERS, lasses, reapers, mowers,
Hedgers, delvers, toilers, sowers,
Come and dance with steps untired:
For this day you are required
To do honour to our queen
Crowned with flowers and rushes green.
Never Maytime did present
Such a wondrous ornament,
No, nor spring the meadows kiss
For a blossom fair as this.
Pray we now that Heaven may shower
All its blessings on her bower,
And that Time may bring her more
Ever to increase her store.
Thus we sing and thus we move
Holy Powers to grant their love.

PHILLIS AND COLIN.

PHILLIS sat upon a bank:
    Heigho, what a bank was this!
Painted blossoms blowing rank
    Round about, each other kiss.

Colin came and sat thereby:
    Heigho, bravest wight was he!
Came and sat with many a sigh:
    Thus fond lovers love to be.

Dearest maid, I now will tell,
    Heigho! all my passion's force,
Deeper than the deepest well,
    Swifter than the river's course.

He said yea, and she said nay:
    Heigho! love is lost and won,
Raging till the weary day,
    Sick of strife lies down fordone.

Then they smiled and kissed again.
    Heigho, Cupid, naughty elf!
If you want another strain,
    You may sing it for yourself.

MAY MORNING.

AS down in yonder vale I went when daffodils were
    springing,
Whereby a crystal stream did go, I heard a maiden
    singing:
And thus she said, My pretty lambs, now is the sun-
    shine weather,
Come let us dance upon the grass with joyous hearts
    together.
    The hoary hawthorn blossoms sweet,
    Gay songsters one another greet,
    Glad voices sing in every street
      To welcome the May morning.

Then setting by my crook, I sped to where the dainty
    creature
Trod on the sward with airy steps the gracious time
    did teach her,
And pray'd my pipe might join her song, and in her
    blithesome tripping,
My frolic step might match with hers; for that the
    prime was slipping.
    And so we sang the song again,
    And danced across the flow'ry plain;
    And as we sang our hearts were fain
      To welcome the May morning.

THE SHEPHERD'S GARDEN.

LOVE A SERGEANT

RUN, gallants, run
   This is Love's own day.
Hark! up and down the street
His rolling drum is beat:
   Rub a dub, rub a dub:
Ye that will come may.

Lo! yonder he doth stand,
His quiver in his hand.
All ye that may be willing
To take his proffered shilling,
   Make no delay,
   But come away
And join his valiant band.

Look, how he doth unfurl
His banner! 'tis a curl
Of auburn flowing hair;
And, for those who love not fair,
He hath of dark a store,
With many colours more:
His shield wears for device
Two pretty shining eyes,

And a heart doth show there too,
With an arrow stricken through.
Oh, his warfare is so sweet
For those who therein meet,
That for very joy they shout
    And they cry,
    Till we die
We will fight the battle out!

Come then, ye gallants, bent
To serve Love's regiment,
Whilst with a loud rebound
His rolling drum doth sound
    Rub a dub, rub a dub,
To all the country round.

THE AWAKENING OF DAPHNE.

DOWN in the dewy woods, 'mid blossoms weeping,
   Daphne, rare Daphne, softly lies a-sleeping.
Come not, Apollo, with thy beams to wake her;
Forbear, ye herald winds, with fear to take her.

Lo! from the shuddering boughs sick Philomel
Drop songless, whilst the larks begin to swell
Their airy quire on rosy wings, and cry,
He comes, he comes: forsake thy couch and fly!
She wakes, she turns, and lightly speeds away,
And soon outstrips the ardent god of day.
The trembling flow'rs for joy and sorrow blush:
Daphne is safe hid in a laurel bush.

THE SWEET SEASON.

COME hither, shepherds, come,
  Now the bees with busy hum,
    And every bird his cheery note doth sing, sing, sing.
Cold Winter he is gone,
Summer sits upon her throne
    Where the rivulets with merry chiming ring.

Upon her head is set
A floral coronet,
    And in her heaped-up hands so fine, fine, fine,
Bright blossoms beam like stars,
And the garment that she wears
    Is broidered with long sprigs of columbine.

See how she sits at ease,
Singing gaily where the trees
    Hang their burdened branches to the ground, ground, ground!
Oh, for love of such a queen
Each joyous heart had been
    With Cupid's thorny wreath of roses crown'd!

TO PAN.

SHEPHERD PAN, who lov'st to play,
On thy oaten pipe all day
Where the singing waters meet,
Lapping round thy horny feet,
Blow into thy reed such sound
Whereto nymphs do beat their ground
When the woods revest their green,
And each shepherd, well beseen,
Holding other cares at call,
Hies him to the festival:
So for thee and more for me
Ours a happy time shall be.

First I ask, my bleating flocks
Thou wilt guide amongst the rocks,
And the tiny lambkins lead
Whilst the dams securely feed,
So the wolf may fall i' th' snare,
And no enemy be there:
And for those who gave me birth,
Aged couple by the hearth,
Let them, through calm life's decline,
Feel the sun more brightly shine,

Loving still whom love begot,
Stars of heaven declining not.

Then I bid thee tune thy quill
To the music of the rill,
Begging there a little boon,
As it wanders stone by stone,
That if near my mistress go,
She may all my passion know,
And not turn her from my bower,
Sweet for her with every flower;
But through tender ways may be
Brought by Love to dwell with me:
Blossom born without a tear,
Clothed with joy that angels wear.

Next my love's most dear perfections
We will trace from our defections:
Eyes which hint the wondrous story
Of the soul's supernal glory,
Ivory teeth, and such a lip
Love himself runs mad to sip,
Hair unfolding wreath by wreath
Subtle gins to snare us with,
That, in faith, you would not know
Any more than I do so,

If there be so fair a creature
In the round of human nature.

Ho! god Pan, swart country singer,
Let not sweet division linger;
Puff thy cheeks until they be
Round as apples on the tree:
Hark the throstle in the dell
Troll his lusty carol well!
Here doth love to roam about
The cuckoo with his merry shout:
And at work amongst the trees,
Cheerful sound of buzzing bees.
This fair kingdom all our own,
Cæsars could not paragon.

Other singers may decry
Mirth and wholesome jollity,
Searching through a musty brain
Matter for some novel strain,
Taxing twisted phrase and vexing
All their soul to vain perplexing,
But instructed wiselier we,
Like the cuckoo on the tree,
Sing the old song to the letter,
For that Time hath found no better,

THE SHEPHERD'S GARDEN.

Nor another theme employs
Worthier than these country joys.

Therefore pipe, brave shepherd Pan;
Blow and quit thee like a man:
Let thy treble take the wind,
And thy bass come swift behind.
This our life doth gaily pass,
Lying in the summer grass,
Where the chirring grasshopper
Keeps around perpetual whirr,
And the sun-sparks burn and glisten
On the leaves that bend to listen,
Whilst the very clouds seem bound,
Pausing at the silvery sound.

Pipe, old Shepherd, pipe thy fill:
I will stead thee to thy will;
I will sing a gallant measure,
Tripping to thy light heart's pleasure.
Howsoe'er thy shrill notes ring,
Thou shalt hear me answering;
Not a strain that thou canst blow
But I will be echo to:
For the fairest joy that is
Lives within this country bliss,

To which all other states that are
Do but hold a base compare.

So may I forsake the strife
And struggle of ambitious life,
I will never cry or crave
Riches more than now I have :
This clear stream and yonder dale
With my cottage in the vale,
Pastures white with nibbling sheep,
Quiet hours that always keep
Counsel of content and learn
How this world doth vainly turn,
Gathering wisdom in such school
Life doth foster fresh and cool.

This I ask, and thus would I
Peaceful live and tranquil die.

A MADRIGAL.

IN fair Arcadia it fell upon a merry morning,
    When Flora's hands the fields and meads with blossoms were adorning,
Phillis sat beside a bank with all her swains around her,
Who, by her lovely looks allured, with wistful steps had found her :
Full silently they sat and sighed, for none did dare discover
The hapless fire that burned within to call himself her lover ;
And one looked up and one looked down, whilst Phillis smiled upon them,
And little birds amongst the boughs with chirpings did bemoan them.
    Then from her throne of rushes,
    She said, with maiden blushes,
The tender wishes of her heart with modesty unmasking,
He shall not bear away the bell who waits to kiss for asking.

ALEXIS' RESOLVE.

SHEPHERD ALEXIS, coming from the town,
  Within the shadow of an oak sat down,
And pondered the inconstant ways of men;
The cuckoo calling down the hollow glen:
Then as the sliding brook ran sweetly by,
He clasped his hands and breathed a happy sigh,
And in his heart with fervent protest swore
To leave these peaceful pastures nevermore.

COUNTRY CONTENTMENTS.

WHO simple faith doth hold his guest,
    And more than turmoil, loveth rest,
Let him forsake all noisy cares,
And come and breathe these country airs.

For silk and pearl, we ask not them,
Whom every bud doth bring a gem;
Our fleecy flocks to us do bear
The useful garments that we wear.

Our board is laid with herbs that grow
Where silver fountains fall and flow;
Our cows with milk, our streams with fish,
Supply the banquet that we wish.

The pretty strawberry so sweet
Doth fit our appetite with meat:
The orient peach and purple plum
To crown our festive triumph come.

The proudest she that wears a gown
Might gladly to this fare come down,
For here sweet Love doth make his feast
Of wholesome food with smilings drest.

Here jolly Momus leads his rout,
And trolls his merry catch about:
With mirth and laughter all agree
Beneath the shade of some wide tree.

Above our heads the bleeding vine
Doth drop our cups with purple wine,
And tendrilled leaves and branches brings
To crown us monarchs more than kings.

Then, when our feasting we have sped,
Some roam the flower-enamelled mead,
And some go forth to dance and play;
Thus keep our rural holiday:

Until the evening star doth rise,
And blossoms close their weary eyes,
Then, pleased, exchange a calm good-night,
To wake at morn with new delight.

THE SHEPHERD TO HIS MISTRESS.

SWEET, whilst the sun is shining,
    Let us put by repining,
        And roam the country round:
        For this is Love's own ground.

For thee morn spreads her posies,
And summer-blowing roses
        With circling odours tell
        The air where thou dost dwell.

Fair crystal streams abiding
Do stay their nimble sliding;
        Whilst every floating fish
        Doth wait upon thy wish.

The fields bring forth the guerdon
Of Flora's teeming burden:
        All hearts are fain to say,
        How sweetly shines the day!

The woods and groves are ringing
With dainty voices singing:
        Each pretty bird doth find
        A love-mate to his mind.

Come then, my fairest, dearest,
Who such a goodness wearest,
    Let love with sweet delight
    All parted pains requite.

DIANA AND ENDYMION.

WHEN the heat of day was done
    Lay forworn Endymion
Pillowed on high Latmos' steep,
Bowed his head in heavy sleep;
All his flocks had gone to rest,
Folded on the mountain's breast:
Then Diana, pale with woe,
For that love consumed her so,
Cast her javelin aside,
Veiled in humbleness her pride,
Came and stooped where he did lie,
Whilst her nymphs were standing by,
Kissed him on the lips and cheek,
Bade him ope his eyes and speak;
Yet although he dreamt of her,
He might never wake or stir;
For should he aroused be,
She must hide beyond the sea.
Very fair indeed she was:
Lover's hearts might cry, alas!
Buskined feet and bravely clad,
Two white stags for steeds she had,
In her hand a bow she bare
A silver crescent graced her hair;

Every nymph that stood her round
With a star of light was crown'd.

Oh, my love is young and sweet:
In her all such beauties meet:
Gems she needs not, for her eyes
Stain the clearness in them lies;
Might she come where I do sleep,
Ere the prying morn doth peep,
Kiss me lovingly, so I
Should dream of such felicity,
And such lands of wonder strike,
Earth can never show the like,
And my soul such rapture take
I might never wish to wake;
Always sleeping in that bliss,
Ravished with an endless kiss!

A MADRIGAL.

ON a fair day, a merry sunshine day,
   I met a dainty nymph, so brave, so brave and gay.
     She spoke unto me, smiling,
     Words of rare beguiling,
   Breathing of the prime and Love's warm leisure:
Let us forth amongst the fields to make glad holiday,
     And crop bright Flora's treasure.
     The lusty season decks the vale
     With blossoms feeding every gale:
       True love is dearest pleasure;
       No other joys may measure.
     Lie we here recounting his sweet tale,
       Whilst birds are chiming over
       Where leafy groves do cover,
       And rivulets replying,
       Make answer at their dying.
         Sing, Happy day:
         Care flies away
           With fa la la!

THE SHEPHERD'S GARDEN.

THE SHEPHERD'S WOOING.

A SHEPHERD sat beneath an oak,
   Oh, the happy wooing!
When as grave Cynthia did unyoke
Her team and bright Apollo woke.
   This was Love's sweet doing.

And by his side beneath the tree,
   Oh, the happy wooing!
Sat a maiden fair to see:
Lips and eyes might well agree.
   This was Love's sweet doing.

When he told his tale, I wis,
   Oh, the happy wooing!
Turning rosy through her bliss,
She did not scorn the proffered kiss.
   This was Love's sweet doing.

So he took his crook, and she—
   Oh, the happy wooing!—
Promised soon his bride to be;
Then, hand in hand with her, said he,
   This is Love's sweet doing.

THE QUARREL.

SOUND up the fife and tabor:
Come join my song, good neighbour,
   With fa la la la la.

Do you then strike the key,
With a measured do, re, mi.
   Fa la la la la.

You sing amiss, good sooth, sir,
'Tis you, 'tis you in truth, sir,
   With your fa la la la la.

Nay, an' we quarrel thus,
Our friends will say to us,
   Fie on your fa la la:
   Fie on your fa la la!

AN INVITATION TO BANISH SADNESS.

HARK! the cowboy blows his horn:
  Hey ho, trolly lolly!
Whilst birds do sing on every thorn,
  And banish melancholy.

The limpid brooks all laughing go;
  Hey ho, trolly lolly!
And balmy winds begin to blow,
  To banish melancholy.

The time doth challenge every care,
  Hey ho, trolly lolly!
To come and sport it in the air,
  And banish melancholy.

On sunny banks glad lovers sit,
  Hey ho, trolly lolly!
And twine the flowers to garlands fit,
  So banish melancholy.

The rustic lad doth set his mind,
  Hey ho, trolly lolly!
To voice his joy on every wind
  And banish melancholy.

The bee is buried in his flower:
    Hey ho, trolly lolly!
Bright blossoms hang on every bower,
    To banish melancholy.

The nimble squirrel lightly hops:
    Hey ho, trolly lolly!
The rabbit leaps about the copse,
    To banish melancholy.

Rejoicing shepherds laugh and sing;
    Hey ho, trolly lolly!
And many a merry measure fling,
    To banish melancholy.

These country swains such pastimes use:
    Hey ho, trolly lolly!
That sorrow hath no time to choose:
    Thus banish melancholy.

THE PENSIVE SHEPHERD.

WHEN hot noon lay on the hill,
    And the feathered quire was still,
I did light me on a nook,
By a willow-shaded brook.
Down I cast me on the bank
Midst the rushes bristling rank.
Round I heard gay voices ring,
Rustic folk a-summering:
But the merry sound they had
Only made my heart more sad:
For I thought on youth's decay,
And that joy must fall away;
And I saw how promise lies
When it comes to touch, and flies:
How the buds we hold to hand
Wither ere their sweets expand,
And what we did wish before,
We may wish for evermore;
For our cheating fancies win
Only shrouds to wrap us in.
Thus I did forswear me then,
Thinking on the ways of men.

THE SHEPHERD'S GARDEN.

Sad with pity, strained with ruth,
All the forecast of my youth;
And this saw I did approve
Fitly made for my behove:
Fairest hopes that Time doth bring
Flit upon the fleetest wing.

THE SHEPHERD'S HOLIDAY.

WHILST Time his glass is turning
    Let us leave off sad mourning;
        Sing we in care's despite
        To welcome glad delight!

Thus Age our sports ensuing,
Shall find Youth's warm renewing;
    And frisk it to and fro
    As round the world we go.

For so the frolic season
Doth bid rejoice with reason.
    Now to the tabor's beat
    Keep time with nimble feet.
                Fal la la!

THE SHEPHERD'S GARDEN.

THE FESTIVAL.

WHEN foxgloves prank the fields about,
    And garth and grove are green,
And from the brook the leaping trout
    To take the fly is seen;
When the milking-maid hath borne her pail
    Amongst the lowing cows,
And fleecy sheep, through hill and dale
    With tinkling bells do browse;
When caws the rook in the old elm-tree,
We shepherds dance and merry be.

So lusty lads and lasses gay
Make feast and jovial holiday:
The world no wealth like this can give
In which we happy rustics live:
    With lover's toys,
    And country joys,
We turn the hours, nor wish for more
Than health and calm contentment's store.
Your land and gold we weigh not a pin,
    As we sing away care with hey down derry:
For love is a pretty thing to win:
    So nymphs and swains be merry.

THE LITTLE BIRD'S SONG.

MY father was a redbreast, my mother was an owl;
    And I will sing a pretty song if you will fill the bowl.
Gaily Johnny goldfinch, bobbing on a thistle,
Hops and dances blithely to the blackbird's merry whistle:
Fink fink, the chaffinch says; chu chu, the nightingale;
And many a merry bird beside doth tell his happy tale;
Tiny Tommy titmouse, chittafa, says he,
The careless cuckoo shouting as he slides from tree to tree;
Dapper little whinchat flitting o'er the hay,
Utick-tick-tick, he doth cry all a summer's day:
Hark, the yellow-hammer his mournful note prolong,
Teru teru teroo, he wails with sorrow in his song:
Caw, cries the robber rook as he flaps across the corn:
Crake crake, the landrail shrieks in the grass at night and morn:
Jove's bird, the little wren, doth tune his tender throat:
Cheep cheep, the silly sparrow hath but a single note.
So here is health and wealth to all, for now I go away:
If you will hear my song again I'll come another day.

TO A SINGING THRUSH.

WHILST through pride of false renown
    Blustering man struts up and down,
And with thoughts of state grows big,
Thou dost perch upon thy twig,
And the joyful season greet
With a note so very sweet
That the woods and streams rejoice
Ravished by thy mellow voice:
Such a music in it lies
Drawn through rarest melodies.

Happy he who loves to listen
When the dews about him glisten,
To the gurgling from the brake
That blithe heart of thine doth make,
Striking those deep chords that lie
Bound in the soul of harmony—
Rapturous breathings softly blown,
Circling the high-lifted throne,
Where great Jove doth hush his thunder,
Sitting in a silent wonder!

I would have, if that the having
Were but fruited in the craving,

And the warbling of thy bill
Such a grosser mean might fill,
A lute of amber, golden strings,
Thus to chime thy carollings;
All thy sweetnesses rehearse,
Melt thy music in my verse,
And those happy thoughts make clear
Wherewith birds delighted are.

I would tell of twilight woods,
And those sylvan solitudes
Muffled from the noonday beam,
Where the lazy lilied stream
Kisses, on its tangled banks,
Blue forget-me-nots in ranks,
And the meadow-sweet breathes out
Almond odours round about:
Sometimes from the distant meads,
Shepherds piping on their reeds.

I would speak of Summer laid
Underneath some elm-tree's shade,
Fields and woods around him lying,
Fleecy clouds above him flying,
When his song is lightly borne
Over fields of waving corn;

Sun and shadow on the copse
Playing with the loose-strife tops :
Not a wild rose blossoming
Dares but dance when he doth sing.

I would follow thee to where
Garden odours fill the air :
Poplars rising straight and tall ;
Apples ripening o'er the wall :
Flutter with the butterflies,
Pick the ripest strawberries,
At the grottoed fountain sip,
Where long fronds of hart's-tongue dip,
Then the rural feast repay
With my longest loudest lay.

With thee I would hold my course
To the river's lonely source,
Where a barren valley wide
Slopes its rocks on either side,
Splintered ash and pine-tree dun
Basking in the glaring sun,
Whilst the shepherd lad doth keep
Watch amongst the scattered sheep ;
Only one white cloud and still
Sleeping on the topmost hill.

If this may not wholly be,
Yet, sweet bird, I'll sing with thee
Such a song the brooklet near
And the wind shall pause to hear:
All our joys in yonder dell
Each to other we will tell;
Thus to make a dainty verse
Carping wits may not asperse;
With such pauses as may feather
Loftier flights of song together.

THE SHEPHERD INVOKES THE WOODLAND BIRD TO TELL HIM OF HIS MISTRESS.

DAINTY sweet bird that sittest on a spray
    Singing in gallant strain the livelong day,
Hast thou not seen a maiden passing fair
Go by this way to take the morning air?
Her step was light as is the thistle-down
By toying zephyrs o'er the meadows blown;
Her hands a silken whiteness showed to view,
Like maps of Paradise enamelled blue
With veinèd rivers: he who kiss them might
Would count himself to reach joy's topmost height.
Within the garden of her face were set
The rose, the lily, and the violet,
Therein did beauty wage a smiling war
Through budding lips of curious cinnabar;
And as for all her tresses orient gold,
My languid art must leave their wealth untold;
Nor fed with inward glory, may my breath
Make air of any slightest word she saith.—
Oh tell me, lusty bird, if thou hast seen
This beauteous goddess that I call my queen;
So may these woods be echo to thy song
Through many a mirthful summer bright and long!

THE SHEPHERD PRAYS HIS MISTRESS TO SPEAK HER AFFECTION.

NAY but thine eye doth tell me what
    Thy cruel lips forswore:
Though Love doth bid dissemble not,
    False shame will lie the more.

Command these sullen fears depart:
    Why shouldst thou do this wrong,
To let the love that burns thy heart
    Freeze on thy silent tongue?

The modesty thy soul would hold
    Shall not affect thee less
Because thy lips shall grow more bold
    Thy passion to confess.

Nor shall I those high laws reject
    Thy niceness writes for thee,
But to thy virtue's fair respect
    More willing servant be.

LOVE'S ALCHEMY.

WHEN Spring first thought to prank the bowers
    And make the fields her own,
Lucilla brought me pale wind-flowers
    That in the woods had grown.

So ravished of her golden touch,
    And taken by her breath,
The woodland zephyrs have not such
    When morning wakeneth.

She gave them, and a dewy tear
    Upon my hand did lie,
Which changed to pearl, and this I wear
    For jewel till I die.

CUPID'S THEFT.

MY rose grew crimson in the bower,
    My fruit hung on the tree,
When thou didst come in evil hour,
    And pluck them all from me.

But think not that thou shalt escape:
    In troth I swear to thee,
For this thy most unconscioned rape,
    Thy pinions clipt shall be.

THE SHEPHERD'S SCORN OF LOVE.

NAY, Love, I scorn and flout thee :
    Look, I can do without thee ;
Nor will the pains discover
Of such a foolish lover
Who knows not that thy dart
Is but a pricking smart
For laughter ; not for tears ;
And such a lightness wears,
The wise man well beseemeth
Who peaceful hours esteemeth ;
Nor lets his spirit down
For thy fantastic frown :
    But to thy bow
    Disdain doth throw,
With, Ha, ha, ha! and Ho, ho, ho!
Such sport was never known.

THE FERRY.

ONE morn I rose right early to get me o'er the ferry,
Whereas I met a fair maid as bonny as a cherry:
Around the happy boat king Neptune's nymphs did
    play:
So Beauty doth embrave it and bear the palm away.
No crown of gold and jewels that ever queen did wear
With her uncrownèd forehead for wonder might com-
    pare.
    With a heave ahoy, boys, heave ho!
        So merrily we go
    Whilst nimble winds the sails do kiss.
        What a brave world is this:
        No joy sweet lovers miss!

MAGNUS DEUS SAPPHO.

THE LIBYAN SAPPHO taught the birds
    To voice his name abroad,
That all who heard their chanted words
    Might know him for a god.

But Livia such sweet grace doth own,
    That every earthly thing,
To make her blest perfections known,
    Doth find a voice to sing.

So rocks and streams and woods and fields
    Are vocal with her name;
Nor any cloud or beam but yields
    Some record of the same.

HERO.

SAD HERO sat beside the tower
    Where young Leander lay,
His hair bedabbled with the shower
    Of ever-falling spray:
She beat her breast, and, passion-moved,
    Cried to the cruel sea,
Since thou hast drowned my heart's beloved,
    My weeping shall drown thee.

Farewell, sweet peace, fond love doth die
    Upon this watery shore,
And here my languid corpse shall lie
    To rise up nevermore:
For when thy grief-grown waves do leap
    Their bounds, O cruel sea,
And not a tear is left to weep,
    I'll drown myself in thee.

JOVE'S CHEAT.

WHEN JUNO crowned her brows with fire,
    And Jove from heaven came down,
His godship, changed by base desire,
    A cuckoo bird had grown :
With tuneful voice he sweetly sang,
While all the woodland round him rang,
Cuckoo, cuckoo! a tender strain
High Juno's heart might not disdain.

But as he fluttered to her breast,
    Cuckoo, he cried in vain :
He might not there set up his nest ;
    She drove him back again :
For when he would repose him there,
And make those lily beds his lair,
Peaw, peaw! the peacock cried,
Whose many eyes the cheat descried.

But now fair Juno sits the queen
    In yonder heaven of light,
Great Jove doth nurse a sullen spleen
    Her softness to requite.

Forbear, he cries, to hear the song
Of that vile bird shall do thee wrong;
And take the peacock to thy side,
Whose many eyes shall be thy guide.

THE IDEAL.

FAIR-BROW'D NARCISSUS, bending where
  A crystal pool did smoothly lie,
Saw in its bosom, pictured clear,
  His soul's ideal to his eye ;
And gazing still, by fancy fed,
With his own charms was ravishèd.

So I, in looking on thy face,
  Do see in wondrous lines exprest,
Through emblem of thy perfect grace,
  The bright ideal of my breast ;
And love myself in loving thee,
Who art the noblest part of me.

CANZONET.

KISS me, fair love, whose kiss fond lips delighteth:
   Where you do kiss no blistering sorrow biteth;
And kissing smile; for in your sunlike smiling
Is such a radiance of divine beguiling
Doth make the earth a garden of fine blisses
Perfumed with flowery odours of your kisses.

CAST AWAY CARE!

NOW is the day we love to see:
    Hark, the bells do ring us round;
Come, nymphs and swains, and merry be,
    And lightly measure out your ground.
        The rebeck's strain
        Doth sound amain.
        If ye love
        Youth's sport to prove,
    Rural satyr, sylvan faun,
    Come and trip it o'er the lawn:
Couple hands and swing about,
Thus to grace our jovial rout:
For that fair Apollo bids
Shepherds leave their lambs and kids,
Fearless any wolf shall dare
This high day forsake his lair.
Therefore sport it while ye may:
Time doth bid all care away.

LOVE WILL FIND A WAY.

SUCH a merry time it was
When gay Flora riched the grass,
With her choicest buds and flowers
Strewing all the hedgerow bowers,
That no single spot was seen
Where her footsteps had not been.
There upon a sheltered stone,
Phillis sat with Corydon.
Bravest prince of swains was he,
Fairest shepherdess was she.
Corydon would steal a kiss,
Which, he said, she could not miss.
Phillis said it was a shame.
Corydon, Love was to blame,
For that he did only sip
What Love offered to his lip;
And that since she was so coy,
He would give her back the toy.
She said swains were saucy-bold.
He said maids were made of gold.
Thus at odds when Love had seen them
Waste the hour, he stepped between them;
Put her hand in his and said,
Lovers quarrel thus to wed.

So he ended all their strife
In the name of man and wife;
And this saying taught that day,
Love will always find a way.

STOP THIEF!

HAVE you seen a lad go by
    Running this way? He had on
A feathered bonnet; and there shone
A magic lightning in his eye:
A bow he carried; on his back
A loaded quiver he did pack;
And in his hand a heart he bare,
Which from my bosom he did tear.
 Sing hey, sing hey, with a heigho!
 Love is an arrant thief I trow:
 Fair blossoms shine on the tree in May:
 This Love hath stolen my heart away.

For so it happened in this wise:
He took me where a pool did lie,
Whereas a youth sat fishing by,
And bade me look into his eyes,
And then by cunning he did creep
Into my breast, where I did keep
This treasure, and with furtive play
Did filch the thing I seek away.
 Sing hey, sing hey, with a heigho!
 Love is a shameless thief I trow:
 Pale blossoms fall from the tree in May:
 Bold Love hath stolen my heart away.

LOVE'S DECEIT.

LOVE came to me one day and brought
   A rose plucked from the tree:
I seized the flower, but little thought
   What bale therein might be.

Within its crimson heart I spied
   A canker-worm did feed;
The thorns which branched from every side
   Did make my fingers bleed.

Then did I pray Love would restore
   The rose back to its tree;
But he would take the flower no more,
   And only laughed at me.

THE INTERDICTION.

TOUCH not that hand more white than snow
   Of lilies in their prime,
Whose odoured sweets fond youth did know
   In backward tracts of time:
A subtle fire therein doth burn,
Thy heedless heart to dust shall turn.

Forbear to kiss, though Love invite,
   Those lips of ruby red,
Whose pinks recall swift summer's flight,
   With perfume that has fled:
So ravishing their sweets do lie
That in their sweetness thou shalt die.

A hand of flame, a poisoned kiss
   Shall do thee such despite,
That where thou dost desire thy bliss
   Thou shalt discern a blight;
And all the anguish thou shalt prove,
And bitter fruits of slighted love.

THE VOW.

I VOW to leave thee, Love, I said,
    Thy thrall no more I'll be.
Come, Love replied, here lay thy head,
    And I will comfort thee.

There as I laid my weeping face
    (My heart with woe was sick)
An arrow standing from the case
    Did sting me to the quick.

Oh, cruel Love, I cried, to pay
    My easy fondness so:
Thou bidst me go when I would stay,
    And stay when I would go.

Thy treacherous lips no more I'll meet,
    By hope abusèd still;
For they are poison when most sweet,
    And honey where they kill.

THE SHEPHERD TO HIS MISTRESS WITH A LUTE.

GO forth, sweet lute, to her I love;
    And when she strikes thee, softly wailing,
Tell her of all the grief I prove,
    And languished sorrows unavailing.

But if her touch should bolder grow,
    And passion seek a livelier token,
Then break thy strings, that she may know
    How my sad heart for her is broken.

THE FORCE OF MUSIC.

STRAIN not those chords whose trembling flow
    Doth drown with frenzy my poor heart—
Whose currents from such fountains grow,
    Whence Love renews his languished smart:
Too softly sad they fall and die,
Emblem of Hope's last fading sigh.

But if thou wilt with music ease
    My pains, translate my passion's book;
And, more the melody to please,
    Bestow the grace of one kind look;
Then wrap my soul in harmony,
And let me through its sweetness die.

THE INCONSTANT.

THY smiles upon thy frowns do wait,
    Thy frowns upon thy smiles attend;
Love bids me enter at the gate,
    Then scorn my entrance doth forefend.
O truly false and falsely true,
What do I gain by loving you?

Thine eyes do give thy lips the lie,
    Thy lips are liars to thine eyes;
Thy stealing glance, now bold, now shy,
    With fickle light doth fall and rise:
Yet I must ask, whilst I pursue,
What do I gain by loving you?

But constant in inconstancy,
    Thy wayward ways in wanton dress
From change to change do swiftly fly
    Through varying shows of doubleness;
That still I say, as still I rue,
What do I gain by loving you?

A little ribbon here displaced,
    A lock disordered to the wind,
And straightway thou with love art graced;
    And straightway I fresh sorrows find:

Yet though I sigh and sorely sue,
What do I gain by loving you?

Thou hast a heart and thou hast none;
  Thou hast a love, but not for me;
And though I turn and would be gone,
  Yet thou my heart wilt not let be;
But holding me with fetters new,
Make all my loss the loving you.

An ignis fatuus of the mire
  That leads the traveller in the slime,
The ashes of a wasted fire,
  The cold inheritance of Time,
The withered blooms last season blew:
These do I gain by loving you.

A barren harvest reaped from tears
  Which in my bosom's depth were sown,
The labour of outwearied years,
  The hapless hope, the grievous groan,
A clouded sky for cloudless blue:
These I do gain by loving you.

A sickness more than any death,
  A death which kills me day by day,
A woful weight of fleeting breath
  That never yet will flit away,

A pain increase of pain doth woo:
All these I gain by loving you.

When Time shall garner to the dust
   This wasting frame, and bid resign
The burden of long hope and trust
   Which choke the life no longer mine,
Then shall I only find my true
And chiefest gain in loving you.

THE SHEPHERD COMPLAINS TO HIS MISTRESS WHEN SHE WILL FOREGO THEIR LOVE.

NAY, prithee, swear not, love, to break
    Those links so long have tied us;
Nor, fools of Time, consent to make
    Our promises deride us:
Such falsehood in those dreams of bliss,
    My soul cannot discover,
As to forego the wonted kiss,
    And say, Sweet Love is over.

The glorious light from thee I took,
    Will not so soon be blinded,
Nor faithful love torn from my book,
    Though thou be falsely minded:
Grace cannot soon so graceless die,
    Nor love forget the lover,
As thus to give our troth the lie,
    By one, Sweet Love is over.

But if thou wilt then have it so,
    Give back the sighs I gave thee,
When thou didst join me vow to vow
    With whispers to enslave me;

And give me back the tears that I
    Have wept thy slights to cover,
With those dear hopes that will not die,
    Or say, Sweet Love is over.

THE TRYST.

THE earth now doth present
 Her beauty to the moon;
Sweet flowers give up their scent
 And singing brooks their tune,
  Sweetheart, sweetheart,
   Why come you not?
  So soon to part:
   True love forgot!

The church clock on the hill
 Doth chide your long delay;
The nightingale is still
 Because you are away.
  Sweetheart, sweetheart,
   Why come you not?
  So soon we part:
   True love forgot!

THE LOST BIRD.

I KEPT a Robin in a cage;
   Full fine of plume he was:
His song could all my griefs assuage
   And make my cares to pass.

Always he tuned his merry throat:
   So sweetly he did sing,
No sprightlier bird with rarer note
   Made ever thicket ring.

When at the time that April calls
   New blossoms on to May,
He, fluttering, burst his wicker walls,
   And swiftly flew away.

Fair maiden bearing garlands forth
   To shepherds on the green,
Tell me if either south or north
   My Robin you have seen.—

I saw in passing by the gate
   That shuts the garden bowers,
A Robin singing to his mate
   Amongst the leaves and flowers.—

Nay, stay one moment ere the throng
    You join, and pray declare,
What said my Robin in his song
    Unto that happy fair.—

He said, he loved your bonny eye,
    And praised your lithesome grace;
But that he liked his liberty
    More than your beauteous face.

He said, although you might not change
    A heart so warm and true,
Yet his from sweet to sweet must range
    As bees in summer do.—

Then lead me to the grove where he
    In happier case doth stir,
And I will lie beneath the tree
    Where he doth sing to her:

And I will bathe the grass beneath
    With tears instead of dew,
And sigh away my careful breath;
    For Love shall die there too.

A COMPLAINT OF THE FALSITY OF TIME.

TRUTH, where dost thou hold thy throne:
  In what region now unknown:
Or hast thou for ever flown,
  That no more we may behold thee?
    Faith is falsed and trust is gone:
    Out, alas! Love make thy moan
  For the lies feigned oaths have told thee.

Fie, bold roses blushing, fie!
For he on your bed did lie
Your languished graces now may die,
  Pining pains shall now forego ye:
    Lilies, roses, every one,
    Pinks and pansies, all are gone;
  Love comes back no more to woo ye.

LOVE'S FUNERAL.

WILL you come to Love's funeral?
   He lies dead in the street;
Black mourners spreading forth his pall
   With saddest tears do greet.
He knew a many songs;
   His soul was filled with joy;
He died slain with a hundred wrongs
   That cruel hearts employ.
      O Love, sweet Love,
         We have loved thee long and true,
           And wilt thou leave us thus, Love,
         Without a last adieu?

He was worn with long wandering
   In sorrow up and down:
His quiver backwards he did fling,
   And tramped through all the town.
Fair maidens kissed and sighed
   Alack! when he went by,
As to himself he softly cried,
   Then laid him down to die.
      O Love, sweet Love,
         Loved more than I can tell,
           And wilt thou leave us thus, Love,
         Nor bid us once farewell?

His lips they were very pale;
   His eyes had lost their fire;
Hushed half untold his tender tale,
   The music of his lyre:
Then as he lay forespent,
   Death came and whispered low,
The hour is past to thee was lent,
   And it is time to go.
     O Love, sweet Love,
       Beloved, but all in vain,
         And art thou gone, indeed, Love,
       To come no more again?

LIPS AND ROSES.

RED roses of whose sweets were made
    The joys with Time foregone,
Whose sharpened spines beneath them laid
    Did sting me to the bone,
Can ye rebloom those hours again,
Compact of happiness and pain?
    No, darlings, no :
    Ye cannot so :
Ye come and go in vain.

Empurpled lips besprent with dew,
    Cool morning's tender boon,
Must those first kisses laid on you
    Consume away at noon?
In vain I would call back again
My languished hours of joy and pain;
    Ye whisper, no ;
    That I but so
Waste all my soul in vain.

CORYDON'S LAMENT.

BESIDE a brook last eve I heard with pity
A rueful shepherd chant this doleful ditty.

    Oh, sing with me a dirge,
      And steep yourselves in woe,
    And clothe you all in serge,
      And sadly weeping go;
    My love that was so sweet,
      Hath left me quite alone;
    No more on earth to meet.
      Alack, poor Corydon!
        I have lost my love, he said,
        She is laid in her death-bed:
        There is no hope for me, poor Corydon.

    Her eyes were clear and bright
      As stars in topmost sky;
    Love set therein his light,
      That you might know them by.
    Her hair was all of gold,
      Her face most fairly shone,
    Her form of finest mould
      From Beauty's self was won.

> I have lost my love, he said,
> She is laid in her death-bed:
> There is no hope for me, poor Corydon.

Her hand with gentle touch
   My own would lightly twine,
Soft as a dove; none such
   Shall ever clasp with mine.
She had an angel grace
   So rare to look upon,
As surely now-a-days
   Such grace is never known.
> I have lost my love, he said,
> She is laid in her death-bed:
> There is no hope for me, poor Corydon.

Oh, careful day! I weep
   In vain from morn to eve,
No tears my heart do steep
   My sorrow may relieve;
Yet here, with many a groan,
   My wasting life shall fade,
Until beside her own,
   My body shall be laid.
> I have lost my love, he said,
> She is laid in her death-bed:
> There is no help for me, poor Corydon.

FUNERAL SONG.

BRING not hither any black,
    Weeping symbols, let them be;
Love so perfect doth not lack
    Gum or incense from the tree.

Sound not any dirge or knell,
    Set aside your grave despairs;
Beauty once with her did dwell
    Now another beauty wears.

Cease your sighing; more for bliss
    Is the passage she doth prove:
Death did kill her with a kiss,
    Not in anger, but in love.

Sweetest flowers hither bring,
    Culled from dewy valleys warm;
Wrap her gently, softly sing:
    She is safe from ill and harm.

White her kerchiefed face; her eyes
    Closed in rest; she doth not stir:
Like a fallen blossom lies
    All the mortal part of her.

Touched to sober stillness now
   Face and form are filled with light:
On her alabaster brow
   Peace doth crown a last good-night.
                Good night!

FOREWARNING.

THOUGH the expectant season pour
    All its blossoms in thy lap,
Look not thou for fruit therefore:
    Fairest hope hath foulest hap.

Nothing in this world is sure:
    All men's ways are up and down:
    He doth reap who hath not sown:
Wisdom folly must endure:
Rain may rot the ripened corn;
    Truth decline before the strong:
Love may die for hate and scorn,
    Wary right for wily wrong.
        Though the expectant season pour
            All its blossoms in thy lap,
        Look not thou for fruit therefore:
            Fairest hope hath foulest hap.

Hues that in the rainbow shine
    Do but beacon other showers:
    Cankers grow in fairest flowers:
Every rose puts forth a spine:

Think not that to-morrow shall
   Bring thee better than to-day;
Whatso now doth thee befal
   Coming winds shall waft away.
     Though the expectant season pour
       All its blossoms in thy lap,
     Look not thou for fruit therefore:
       Fairest hope hath foulest hap.

Wealth when gained hath still a dearth:
   Grace by honour is befooled.
   Wouldst thou rule? then thou art ruled:
Count thy gold, it turns to earth:
Kisses are not worth a thought;
   Less than nothing they must be:
Love itself is dearly bought
   With a false felicity.
     Though the expectant season pour
       All its blossoms in thy lap,
     Look not thou for fruit therefore:
       Fairest hope hath foulest hap.

Thus the hollow world doth cheat
   All its votaries one by one:
   Each doth seek to hold his own;
Fraud with falsehood to compete:

Promises are made of air :
Friendship is a gilded face :
Smiles but hide a heart of care ;
Sweetest simpers sour grimace.
Though the expectant season pour
All its blossoms in thy lap,
Look not thou for fruit therefore :
Fairest hope hath foulest hap.

LOVE'S STRATAGEM.

LOVE leading by, one stormy day,
　　Pale Sorrow, wet and worn,
Implored that he with me might stay
　　Until the morrow morn.

And so I took him weeping home,
　　And soothed his throbbing pain;
And then I begged that Love would come
　　And take him back again.

But though I prayed with many a sigh
　　And shook the doleful air,
He would not deign to make reply,
　　Or list to my despair.

And so from day to day I grieve
　　And make perpetual moan;
For Love hath given sad Sorrow leave
　　To call my heart his own.

COUNSEL TO THE LOVER OF A LIGHT MISTRESS.

THOU hapless lover, born to kiss
    The shadow of a vacant bliss
With bitter tears that still do flow,
If thou wouldst wearying sorrow miss,
    Bid Love farewell, and let him go.

There is no worth in womankind
To leave thy wealth of peace behind;
    For though her beauties thou may'st know,
Yet who shall all her failings find?
    Then give good-bye, and let her go.

If thou with prayers and tears wilt try
To gain her graces presently,
    Think not to reach those favours so;
For she will lightly pass them by:
    Then bid farewell, and let her go.

What thou dost wish she will refuse,
What thou wilt not that will she choose;
    She smiles when as thy tears do flow;
Thy love and faith she will abuse:
    Then bid good-bye, and let her go.

Think not because her cruelty
Is subtly hid from every eye,
   Her heart doth any pity know,
Whose very sweetness is a lie;
   But say good-bye, and let her go.

Though she her favours freely fling
It is not for remembering;
   For she will flout both high and low,
And of their woes will gaily sing;
   So give good-bye, and let her go.

Trust not her eyes, although they look
Into thy soul as in a book:
   Their light is but a lamp to show
The bait upon the biting hook;
   But give good-bye, and let her go.

What though Love's wing do lightly stir
At every sugared breath of her,
   And when she speaks he bend his bow,
Hold not her wiles thy lawgiver;
   But bid good-bye, and let her go.

Should she with smiles and tears together,
Protest to love through every weather

Whilst stars are bright and winds do blow,
Yet weigh not thou her words a feather;
  But say good-bye, and let her go.

Far better thou shouldst hold thee one
Whom Love denies, than mope and moan
  For her whom Love can never know:
Then leave those icy sweets alone:
  Say once good-bye, and let her go.

Nor grieve thee if she break her faith;
Sworn and despisèd in a breath,
  But count it gain to lose her so;
And Love shall gladden at his death
  To say farewell and let her go.

LOVE'S REPAYING.

HO! Thyrsis, shepherd swain, in grief reclining
    Beneath the willows' shade with vain regarding,
Tear off the cypress wreath thy brows entwining,
    For now thy bitter love hath sweet rewarding.
Hark! how the mellow throstle so doth chaunt it,
Whilst Flora on the emblazoned fields doth flaunt it:
    For love doth come and go,
    As all wise lovers know;
And he who lacks to-day to-morrow shall not want it.

    Thus Daphne sang to Thyrsis, well relenting
    Of long disdain; with most divine accenting
Bidding the shepherdesses bring her flowers,
That she might wed with him amongst the bowers;
    And so, all scorn dismissing,
Did end his sorrows with her sweetest kissing.

CUPID'S TREACHERY.

CUPID lay tumbling in a rose,
    When Celia caught him,
Filled with soft warmth a sweet repose
    Had gently brought him:
Then did she lay her bosom bare,
And lightly bid him welcome there;
    For she had sought him.

So long he lay hushed on her heart,
    It were a wonder;
Then did he draw a pointed dart
    So deep did wound her,
That by the wings she plucked the god,
    And quickly stript him,
And taking up a myrtle rod,
    She soundly whipt him
Until he cried for pity, then
She coaxed him into smiles again;
With tender words she soothed his pain,
    And sweetly lipp'd him.

O Love, and has my Celia found for thee
A heart of pity, yet hath none for me?

THE SHEPHERD'S GARDEN.

ALL THINGS TO MY LOVE AM I.

I CAN laugh and I can cry :
   All things to my love am I.

Dost thou love, then I love too;
Art thou cold, I will not woo :
Wouldst thou sunlike smilings show,
Then all frowns I will forego ;
Or if thou wilt frown awhile,
I will banish every smile :
If thy lips are turned to me,
Then my kisses wait on thee ;
Or if thou say no to them,
Then such toys I will contemn.
   I will laugh or I will cry :
   All things to my love am I.

Art thou silent, and would rise
On wings of high philosophies,
Then my sober judgment broods
With thee in those beatitudes ;
Or if thou dost laugh and talk,
Amorous in the woodland walk,
Still my heart with thine shall dance
In love's delightful dalliance :

Or if thou wouldst carol it,
My song with thine shall rarely fit.
   I will live or I will die :
   All things to my love am I.

Give me foul or give me fair,
I will match thee to a hair :
Give me foul or give me fine,
Yet my mood shall equal thine :
If thy lips shall breathe me, Yea,
Bound to thee my faith shall stay :
Or if thou do say me, No,
I will bid farewell and go,
Ranging like a summer bee
Where the sweets are still for me.
   Laugh or cry, or live or die :
   All things to my love am I.

THE SHEPHERD RIDICULES THE FALSE CHARMS OF A
FLAUNTING BEAUTY.

MY lady's glance the world doth bless
   With love-diffusing light,
When that she hath no waywardness
   And is not curst with spite.

Rich hair she hath and smoothly laid,
   In golden fillet bound;
And all her own; for it was paid
   With yellow gold and round.

Her lips are red as winter haws:
   No wanton kiss may taint
Their modest innocence, because
   Their hues are laid in paint.

Her hand is white if that it be
   Cased in a satin glove;
And all the Graces go when she
   With gracious step doth move.

Her eyes within her mirrored glass
   Her own heart's love do take:
Her blooming cheeks are rosy as
   Vermilion can make.

Her nose to scorn her cheeks would wear
   A ruddier glow than they,
If that it did not mainly fear
   To melt in flames away.

Her arching brows are fixed in jet
   Stroked through a cunning dye:
Love smiles to see her smilings set
   In teeth of ivory.

So by her Art the world we see
   Of every grace bereft,
That beggared Nature groans to be
   Without a beauty left.

WOOING AND WEDDING.

I LEANED upon a meadow's gate,
   And watched the waving grass,
When spring with warmer suns doth mate,
   And into summer pass.

And there I saw two lovers go
   Along the spangled mead,
Whereby a singing stream did flow
   Half hid in rush and reed.

They whispered words of sweet consent;
   Each held the other's hand:
Love breathed the wind that round them went,
   And bloomed the flowery land.—

At autumntide I passed that way
   When they were man and wife;
But all their toys and loving play
   Were turned to married strife.

The thrush sang vainly on the hill,
   The blackbird piped unheard:
Yet, as they wrangled loudly, still
   She had the latest word.

Then as those songsters frighted flew,
This rhyme rang in my head:
Fair maidens who are sweet to woo
May yet be sour to wed.

THE STRIFE.

IN happy ease, down in a pleasant vale,
  Where nibbling sheep bestrewed the neighbouring
    plain,
Beside a gurgling brook, whose undersong
Lulled all the woodland to a still repose,
Two shepherds sat, and played upon their pipes,
And sang by turns in friendly strife; and one
Would give an oaken cup with nymph and faun
And rustic revel carven, one a kid
New washed and white as snow on Ida's top,
To him who should be victor. On a staff
The old Menalcas leaned and smiled, his beard
Flowing in ample grey about his breast:
He umpire chosen. Thus the shepherds sang.

Thyrsis.

My mistress is so fair, I swear her face
  Might make a mirror for the eyes of morn.

Amyntas.

My mistress queens it with so royal grace,
  That royalty itself is left forlorn.

Thyrsis.

Such odours linger round Lucilla's cot,
  Would rob the breath of any rose that blooms.

Amyntas.

Olympia's lilies every fair would blot,
   And blow a garden in the dust of tombs.

Thyrsis.

Lucilla smiles, and all the world is gay,
   And every bird doth praise her on the tree.

Amyntas.

Olympia's wiles chase every care away,
   And where she dwells is happiness to be.

Thyrsis.

Lucilla's beauty shines so eminent,
   The moon grows dim within the midnight sky.

Amyntas.

Olympia's glance so lights the firmament
   The sun is fain to hide, eclipsed thereby.

Thyrsis.

Rejoice, my flock, and frisk it o'er the lea:
   There is no joy like this the summer yields.

Amyntas.

Leap, little lambs, and show ye merry be,
   Whilst Flora sows her casket on the fields.

Thyrsis.

Run, rivers: fountains fall, and streams be glad:
  Now is the season of our prime delight.

Amyntas.

Blow wind and clash the leaves: no heart is sad
  Which these green hills do shut from worldly spite.

Thyrsis.

This is the crown of life, to sit and sing
  Amongst the meadows when the day is fair.

Amyntas.

Shout, jolly shepherd: hark, the blackbird sing
  His song to make us blithe and free from care!

And then they ceased. But old Menalcas said
Such proof is this, I know not which is best:
So you shall give the cup, and you the kid;
And both content shall lead their flocks to fold:
For now fair Venus sets her star afront,
And weary Apollo scarcely sits his wain
For very heaviness; and only stays
To say good-night and go: so let us go;
And when cool hours have dewed our lids with sleep,
Awake the morrow with as sweet a song.

CERES' TRIUMPH.

FAIR Ceres now doth crown her reign:
　　Set on sheaves of golden grain
　　　　Enthronèd she.
Reapers singing cheerily,
Maidens springing merrily,
　　　　Right gladsome be.
Hark, the sprightly rebeck sound
With scattered echoes round and round,
　　Still ringing high and higher.
Tripping, slipping o'er the ground
Each shepherd maid now joys to see
　　　　Her rustic dancing by her.

THE SONG OF THE PLOUGH.

ALL ye who love good cheer to prove,
    And hold ye to the toast,
Through good and ill, with a gallant will,
    That mirth should rule the roast,
With generous hearts now take your parts,
    As ever ye hope to wive,
And join with me this song in glee,
    God make the plough to thrive!

Ere we were born, when wholesome corn
    Was hard to get and grind,
Our sires that wrought, this maxim taught,
    For us to keep in mind:
If you would gain from toil and pain,
    Or ever you sow and mow,
Be up and away at break of day,
    And learn to follow the plough.

Here's ploughman John, a merrier one
    You will not readily find,
As he follows the plough, his cares, I trow,
    Are left in the furrow behind.

He doth discern, and wisely learn,
    How lords at last must bow,
And soon or late must meet their fate,
    As the stubble by the plough.

His purse is small, for his hands were all
    The wealth at birth he got;
But he has a house and a faithful spouse,
    With something to put in the pot:
And Heaven hath sent him sweet content,
    That he might teach us how
One happy may be as poor as he,
    As he whistles behind the plough.

Your bustling cit he counts no whit
    Of worthier metal made,
Though he may be more rich than he
    Who follows the ploughman's trade:
For though he bear more costly wear
    And equipage enow,
He doth not stand so firm in land
    As he who follows the plough.

The king may groan upon his throne,
    The statesman care may take:
When labour is done, we sleep with the sun,
    And with the sun awake.

Says gaffer, Arise! and gammer she cries,
  'Tis milking-time I vow;
And John must go, with Peter also,
  To follow the thrifty plough!

This pledge I vow, Success to the plough:
  With ribbons it shall be tied,
And Kenneth and Hugh, with Kate and Sue,
  Shall bravely dance beside:
And Joan and Ann, with Bess and Nan,
  Shall join and lightly go,
Each with her lad to make her glad,
  And sing, God speed the plough!

Now have ye grace, each in his place,
  Scorn not this song of mine:
Abundant cheer, with home-brewed beer,
  Be every day to dine:
And ye who love good hap to prove,
  Come carol my chorus now:
A witch's ban light on the man
  Sings not, God speed the plough!

THE DEATH OF SUMMER.

HARK! through the woods the wind doth wail:
    Fair Summer he is dead.
Stick his couch with the poplar pale,
    Ere all its plumes be shed;
With withered leaves bestrew his pall—
Those tears the mourning woods let fall.

Now let sweet robin softly sing,
    From a bare branch alone,
His doleful song at evening,
    When winds have ceased to moan.
Summer is dead: alas! he lies
Stretched on the ground with curtained eyes.

Sad rivers sobbing onward go,
    Cold brooks their course do urge,
Brimming their wasted banks with woe
    To sing sweet Summer's dirge.
Summer is dead: he lies, alas!
Stretched out upon the meadow's grass.

WINTER.

YE fields that were so green;
    Ye meadows strewed with flowers;
Your lustre all so well beseen
    When summer crowned the bowers:

Your sweetness now is reft;
    Your rills hard frost doth seal:
No more the wind, with gentle theft,
    Their music comes to steal.

The flocks in silent bands
    Stand on the banks forlorn,
Whilst shivering shepherds blow their hands
    Beside the naked thorn.

No more glad children stray
    The lanes at even-time;
Where merry feet did dance and play
    Is whitened o'er with rime.

The flowers that once did bloom
    To glad the rustic's toil,
Long since have sought a sullen tomb
    Shut in the frozen soil.

Thus doth the summer pass
With all its joys full soon,
And gloomy night bedims, alas!
Our day before its noon.

THE YULE-TIDE MESSAGE.

WHEN baffled travellers go astray,
   Perplexed upon the whitened heath,
And cottage lights with feeble ray
   Gleam faintly through the misty breath;
When worn-out daylight woos the dark,
And fretful hounds are heard to bark,
And, toiling through the heavy snow,
The muffled waggoner doth go;
When lanes are choked, and woods are bowed,
And streams are hushed in icy shroud,
And whooping owls begin to sail,
And threshers rest the weary flail,
And dormice dream, and birds are fain
To hide them from chill winter's pain;
When noisy school-boys slide the pond,
And whispering lovers grow more fond,
And logs are heaped upon the fire,
And mirth and frolic glee conspire:
     Why, then the time doth bring
     New joys and call to sing,
     Hark around, boys, hark around,
     With what a welcome sound
     Old Christmas-tide doth blow
     His bugles o'er the snow,

And bid us all be merry,
With voices glad and cheery;
Singing, Heigh with a heigho! be merry, boys, be merry!

WELCOME TO CHRISTMAS.

OLD Christmas is come with fife and with drum,
   So let us forget the foul weather:
Though his beard may be white, his warm heart shall
     requite
   All the cold as we trip it together.
We will dance in a ring, we will laugh and will sing,
   To greet the blithe season and merry;
Above us shall grow the green mistletoe,
   And holly shall bring his red berry.
     Here's Polly, Kate, Margery, Phœbe, and Bess,
       With Annot so slender and tall,
     And Cicely fair seen, of beauties the queen:
       So, lovers, come choose for the ball.

Now stir up the fire and let it burn higher,
   Of faggots and logs there are plenty;
Set the candles aflame, for it is no shame
   This festival night to burn twenty.
Let the tabors begin with musical din,
   And light feet be airily glancing:
Grave sorrow despairs to touch the grey hairs
   That shake in this jovial dancing.

Come Polly, Kate, Margery, Phœbe, and Bess,
    Come Annot and lead out the ball:
Sweet Cicely for me my partner shall be,
    For so I will choose from them all.

Now let the dance thrive and mirth be alive;
    And if lads, the coy lasses deceiving,
'Neath the brave mistletoe a kiss should bestow,
    Why, let them not say it is thieving.
Love will not refuse such delicate dues,
    Nor will he be scorned at the flouting;
So maidens despise to cloud your bright eyes,
    And spoil your fair faces by pouting.
    Hey, Polly, Kate, Margery, Phœbe, and Bess,
        Hey, Annot so graceful and tall!
    With Cicely I go through the world high and low;
        For she is the pride of them all.

Though ye hear the cock crow from over the snow,
    Think not that the dawn is advancing;
He doth but rejoice at the cheerful noise,
    Our holiday revels enhancing.
So have ye no care that morning should dare
    To break off our sports in the middle:
Should he show forth his head we will put him to bed
    To the sound of the fife and the fiddle.

Dance Polly, Kate, Margery, Phœbe, and Bess,
  Dance Annot and frisk out the ball :
Brave Cicely my belle shall foot it full well ;
  For she is the deftest of all.

A CHRISTMAS CAROL.

GOOD neighbours old and young, who love this jovial season,
Cast all your care aside and join the feast with reason:
The shrilly pipe doth sound, each rustic beats the ground
With many a leap and bound; such jolly hearts are found:
  For merry Christmas comes but once a year.

All things do find a place to guard them from the weather,
Whilst we with ancient use do trip it all together:
The weary beggar old doth shield him from the cold,
The sheep are in the fold, the dormouse snugly roll'd:
  For merry Christmas comes but once a year.

Money is a good if that we do spend it,
Time doth bid us use, the whilst his grace doth lend it;
Favour will decay, youth will soon away,
The wisest sage doth say, Be happy whilst you may:
  For merry Christmas comes but once a year.

THE SHEPHERD RENOUNCES HIS YOUTHFUL FANCIES.

COME in, ye wandering powers,
    That all my life have been
Like butterflies in April bowers
    When Time was fresh and green.
Tamed by the course of years,
    Ye may not live to scorn
The baptism of those common tears
    To which mankind was born.

Bring here your withered lies
    Unto this funeral pyre,
Wherefrom new-fledged hopes may rise
    Of loftier desire.
Let pride despise his throne,
    And sit upon the ground:
Let selfishness forsake his own,
    And to his friends abound.

Lay all your lusts aside:
    Your foolish whims decrease:
To nobler purposes allied,
    Let wanton follies cease.

Let passion wait on calm:
    Let youthful noise be still:
And for the lover's song, the psalm
    Smooth up the fretted will.

Behold the heavenly feast
    Upon God's table shine,
Whereat, by Reason's graces blest,
    High Wisdom's children dine.
This is that place of love
    Of which the sages tell;
This gilds those palaces above
    Wherein the angels dwell.

MUTABILITY.

I MET with snowdrops growing in a cleft,
Ere yet the snow had left
Their chilly couch, and asked them of the reason.
They did not bide a more congenial season.
They told me they were only harbingers,
Pluming their funeral hearse:
For daffodils were waiting in their wake,
And they must quickly perish for their sake.

Then I did turn to daffodils that stood
Weeping beside a wood,
And prayed them say, why so their bells did ring
Such woful dirge of jaundiced sorrowing,
When all the happy woods and fields were seen
To don their summer's green:
They told me that they mourned their swift decay,
For roses soon should steal their gold away.

Then did I call on roses blushing red,
With their own colours fed,
Love's couch and cradle, and demanded why
They let their loosened petals fall and lie

Plaything of every wind that wantoned there
With rough unmannered air:
They said they were but painted heralds come
To lead in summer's last chrysanthemum.

So passing where chrysanthemums were set,
With tears of evening wet,
I asked why those bright glories I might know
But so short time ere that their light should go
And leave the world bereft of every bloom,
A dark and frozen tomb:
Then did they say, We fade to signify
That all the goodly things of earth must die.

O soul, I cried, and shall thy season's flower
But blow a single hour,
Then fall as these do fall, and fade away;
Thy hope crushed down to make a little clay?
Then did my soul look up, and soon reply,
The flower may drop and die,
But my immortal fruit shall hang on me
Though death should tear the blossom from the tree.

THE EPITOME.

A LITTLE ease, a little fame,
　　A little breath of praise and blame,
A glint of hope by time deceived,
A cloud of falsenesses believed,
A waft of joy, a world of care,
A spark of bliss, a blank despair,
A day of toil, a night of thought,
A wisdom by deep suffering bought,
A battle from whose labouring plain
Resound the cries of woe and pain,
A summer swift, a winter long,
A faith abused by fraud and wrong,
A subtle pang of pain in joy,
A want in wealth, in gold alloy,
A yearning for the better light
Sent up through shades of darksome night:
Lo, here the life we mortals have
Between the cradle and the grave.

THE SHEPHERD WILL FOLLOW HIS BEST MISTRESS, VIRTUE,
WHEREVER SHE MAY LEAD HIM.

THOUGH thou fly me I will follow;
    Thou shalt not forsake me so:
Think not I, by plain or hollow,
    Ever will thy steps forego:
I will be where thou art found;
Faithful love shall track thy ground.

Hear it, hills and dales and fountains,
    Love can blossom dusty graves;
He can level mighty mountains,
    Tame the storms and tie the waves;
He can travel sea or land:
Nothing may his force withstand.

Therefore think not to bereave me
    Of this hope I hold as mine:
Though for starry thrones thou leave me.
    I will mount where thou dost shine,
Enter thy desirèd sight,
Drink the glory of thy light.

THE SHEPHERD UNDER THE FIGURE OF A FAIR MISTRESS PRAISES DIVINE PHILOSOPHY.

SHEPHERD swains whose pipes do please
   Charms of your fair mistresses;
Sylvan, rustic, nymph and faun;
You who nimbly trip the lawn,
Your soft sports awhile forbear,
Whilst I fill the ravished air
With the praise of one I know,
Fairest of all fairs below,
Which I now set forth to tell;
Though I know, and know full well,
That no pipe of mortal touch,
Howsoever sweet; nor such
Music fell from Orpheus' strings,
When he charmed all mortal things;
Nor Apollo's trembling wire,
Thrilled with fine electric fire;
Nor the nightingale at night,
Singing in her love's despite;
Nor the wind that shakes the trees
In embowered Hesperides;
Nor low voice of Siren's tongue,
When she to Ulysses sung;

No, nor anything at all,
Her full sweetness may recall,
Or her high perfections tell,
Whom I do esteem so well.

Yet I will not do her wrong,
Though I lose my name in song,
To forego her praises, when
Less are sung of other men.
He who to the sun would fly,
If he may not reach so high,
Other ventures shall outgo
Which do only aim more low—
Though he partly waste his pain,
Nor can master every grain,
Who would grasp the fleeting sand,
Something stays within his hand:
So my verse, however weak
Her unbounded grace to speak,
Gives me safely to infer
Somewhat may be sung of her.

If you know what 'tis to be
Kissed by blossoms from the tree
When warm June doth throw them down
From the branch where they have grown,

Whilst the gurgling throstles sing
Through the stems at evening,
And a little breeze or so
Lightly thro' the leaves doth go,
You may partly tell, 'tis true,
What a softened touch can do,
Proving, whilst the cool dew slips,
Honeyed taste of dryad lips;
Yet from that to think you are
Of her daintiness aware,
Or therefore can understand
Silken fall of her soft hand,
Would but lead fair truth astray
From the straightness of his way,
Seeing that her gentle ways
Are beyond the reach of praise.

Should ye tell me what delights
Linger out on moonlit nights,
When fond lovers wander where
Sugared murmurs fill the air,
And the stars that o'er them glisten
Stoop their shining heads to listen,
Grottoed brooks and bending trees
Charged with their felicities;
Or if you would bid me lean
Where a river flows between

Sloping banks of velvet grass
Whilst a snow-white swan doth pass
Singing as he floats along
With a flute-like undersong
(Water-lilies round him blown)
Till the wave doth suck him down:
Or if you will tell me what
Happy thoughts were those that brought
Cupid to his Psyche's door
When she dwelt on Love's own shore,
Or what words were those he said
As he kissed her golden head,
And the world itself stood still
Whispered love might breathe his fill: -
These beside the joys I speak,
Are but languid, faint and weak;
Customs half foregone in using;
Faded toys of Time's abusing;
Shrivelled lilies; last year's leaves;
Roses chill October grieves;
Clouds of winters vanished; snow
Filled the fields of long ago;
Sickly pleasures overripe;
Music of a broken pipe;
Errant cheats for which we moan,
Melted, faded, withered, gone.

But the feasts which she doth bring
Ever from pure nectar's spring,
In their wealth perpetual,
Cannot ever cloy or pall,
Filling with enlarged delights
Those diviner appetites
Which immortal souls do prove
Yearning for celestial Love,
Whose uplifted brows and eyes,
Tenants of the topmost skies,
Bring such glory to us down,
Earth would seem to heaven have grown.

Vain it were to touch her worth,
Setting her fair features forth;
Much less her least virtue show
By the tying of a bow,
Or her comeliness express
In the folding of a dress,
Since these scarcely symbolize
Half the worth that in her lies;
Yet I will not stay my verse
From these poor delights of hers,
Made more glorious to the sight
By bright beams of inward light,
Whose clear shafts of heavenly hues
All those others interfuse.

She hath a form full lithe and trim,
Seemly shape and perfect limb,
Dainty lips a little red,
As the rose on them had bled,
Pouting from its thorny tree
At the biting of a bee;
Eyes so bright, that they do bring
Sunny messages to spring;
Hands so perfect in their making
Reach a favour in the taking:
So each well-proportioned grace
Strives the other to outface,
Baffled judgment doth protest
That the latest seen is best,
And confesses her to be
Nature's last epitome.
Might you but these wonders view
By a little glimpse or two,
You would say, and well you might,
Whatsoever of delight
Brought you once the name of bliss,
Was but type and show of this:
For all other joys that are,
Howsoever good or fair,
By her light must quickly own
Touch of some defection,

And be fain to hie them hence,
Stained by her clear excellence.

Though you use the stars at night
To set forth the lovely sight,
Or the flower that brings the day,
When each bird begins his lay,
To make good the joys that lie
In the bounty of her eye,
Yet you shall not know what grace
Meets within her sweet-like face,
Index of a soul so pure
Hope doth fix and sorrow cure;
No, nor yet from these be able
To discern how comfortable
Is the counsel she doth give
To those souls with her do live,
Raising them from earthly things
To the noble rank of kings.

Many a time when I was young,
Fields of blossoms I have sung;
Hawthorn garlands perfuming
Green hedgerows at touch of spring;
Meadows filled with scented hay;
Pleasures of a summer's day;

Nooks of hazel; banks of fern;
Grassy ways that wind and turn;
Airy sweeps the swallow makes
Skimming o'er smooth-bosomed lakes;
Movements of the silvery swan
Leda loved to look upon,
Till his daring bolder grown,
Fired her passion with his own;
Ancient woods whose twilight halls
Echo with white waterfalls;
Russet orchards fruited ripe;
Mellow strains of shepherd's pipe;
Breezy hollows starr'd with flowers;
Country pastimes in the bowers;
Maiden charms so very fair
Might with goddesses compare :—
Yet I now protest that these,
In her absence fail to please,
Nor my soul to rapture move,
If she do withhold her love.

Shepherds in these mountains born,
Take my song at earliest morn,
When the stretchèd daylight lingers
Longest for sweet summer singers:
Chant it to the swelling hills;
Chant it to the lapsing rills;

Chant it in those aisles of green
Forest stems do show between;
Chant it to the flowers that close
When the ruddy evening goes:
So when as the stars do glisten,
If thereto my lady listen,
I shall not desire to wear
Other laurels, or to share
Honours more than she doth bring
To my numbers whilst I sing,
Or the fruit Alcides won
In those gardens of the sun,
Or the fleece of beaten gold
Jason stole from Colchis old:
For her love to me doth crown
More than titled monarch's own,
Who all worldly worth doth praise
With the wonder of her ways.

Therefore, shepherds, celebrate
This my Lady's lofty state,
Till the tongues of men declare
Never one was made so fair,
Or so worthy to have been
Honoured by the name of Queen.

THE LOVE OF THE HIGHEST.

IF I have ever loved in time before,
    Now I love more,
And count all other former loves to bend
    But to this end,
As many roads that lead to one wished place
Where some high towered city lifts his face,
    And gazes at the sun,
Undarkened by the clouds that round him run.

Since I do all thy glories once behold,
    My soul is bold
To leave the vestiges of sodden clay
    For open way,
Winged by the flight of thy far-soaring soul
That bids me touch thy heaven as topmost goal;
    Nor ever sigh or grieve
For these unworthy baubles which I leave.

So teach me how, through many a faithful hour
    To reach thy bower—
To mix my soul with thine, whilst thou dost prove
    Large wealth of love,

Giving me patience and such strength to climb,
That I may smile from those pure heights sublime,
   And keep me safe and clear
From toys that bind men slaves of folly here.

RETIREMENT.

WITHIN these woodland walks and dells
    My sober mind contented dwells,
Where nodding bells do gently close
The drowsy day to soft repose,
And lowing kine and bleating sheep
With prattling brooks sweet concert keep,
Whilst murmured breathings softly blent,
Of winds beneath the firmament,
Blow on the brow with such a bliss
As though they brought an angel's kiss.

When in the morning of the skies
The glorious sun makes haste to rise,
My soul doth run on nimble feet
His early messages to greet,
And on the hillside meet him so
As amorous swains their mistress do;
Or where his chequered radiance flows
Between the lattice of the boughs,
From brightness of his beams I draw
Clear light to read great Nature's law,
And keep my solemn chapel there,
Beyond the noisy ways of care,

Nor harp, nor organ do I need
My soul's religious flame to feed,
Whilst larks, sweet heralds of the sun,
Do up their skyward ladder run,
And swiftly climb the heavenward stair
Thro' the blue circuit of the air,
With such a crowding note to note
Of warbled sweetness from each throat
As bears my praise on mounting wing
Where shining choirs of angels sing,
And rain soft showers of music down
Great Orpheus' lute might sweetly drown.

Here I do make my still delight
To mark the swallow's easy flight;
Or lingering near the stream hard by,
I watch the wanton dragon-fly,
Or gadding water-insects play,
With legs for oars to push their way,
Whilst underneath the silvery tide
The sportive fishes swiftly glide;
From dandelion heads I blow
The hours, and smile to see them go:
I sip my golden liquor up
From chalice of the buttercup,
And on the rose's petals kiss
The rosy lips I do not miss;

The daisy brightens to my eyes
The lights that beauty most doth prize,
Whilst honeysuckles deck their bloom
My spacious chambers to perfume;
My halls are hung with diaper,
And bordered round with oak and fir;
The bending beech, the poplar high,
Do picture forth my tapestry;
Their purple robes the foxgloves bring,
With shooting bays to crown me king:
No softer carpet than the grass
Whereon my royal feet do pass:
Nor want of praisers shall there be,
Whilst courtier birds on every tree
With odes and idyls celebrate
The happy freedom of our state.

Here I do plead with rooks and daws
The justice of my sylvan cause;
My merchant ventures here send forth
Untrembling for the boisterous north;
And in the spirit's better health
Compose my glorious commonwealth;
Amongst these mossy rocks and stones
I marshal my battalions;
And muster all my forces out,
Ambitious discontents to rout;

Counting those laurels best to win
Which make their victories within :
My soldiers, poppies round me spread.
Do range themselves in martial red ;
Tall loosestrifes bending in the vale
Unroll my banner to the gale ;
My pursuivants and men at arms,
The willows bristling by the farms ;
And for my lance, with pennon'd wand,
The bulrush offers to my hand ;
My trumpeter the gallant thrush,
Sounds out the onset from the bush ;
The woodpecker a-pecking comes
With mimic beat of rolling drums ;
Then for the roar of guns I hear
The cuckoo calling loud and clear ;
For cries of woe and sighs of pain,
The chirping grasshopper's refrain.
Thus armed by every element
I storm the forts of discontent ;
Or fight upon the bloodless field
Till rebel-born ambitions yield ;
Or in my mind entrench me well
To keep my bastioned citadel
From fierce attacks of fell desire
For gold, and strife of passion's fire.

Here captain Will doth hold me sure,
And make me dwell therein secure :
Content the door doth lock and clamp,
Whilst Cheerfulness doth light my lamp,
And bid me oft, calm thoughts to feed,
Unclasp Reflection's book to read.

From leafy pulpits I do reach
More truth than schoolmen know to teach,
And, writ in floral tomes, discern
What bookish sages hardly learn.
So fine the meditative act,
It makes a thought become a fact ;
Translates the language of the beech
Into a tongue the mind can reach ;
And through the oak's contorted bars,
Inducts its progress to the stars ;
Interprets, clearly understood,
The brook amongst the underwood ;
And in the river's mellow noise
Rejoices with unfettered voice.

Thick limes across the emerald glade
Spread forth their arms to make me shade,
Whose wandering sweets outdo beneath
The perfumed air that lovers breathe.

To serve me at my wished commands,
The bushes stretch their laden hands;
Green filberts plump their shells and fill
Their husky cases to the frill:
And blackberries distain their lips,
Self-proffered from the bramble tips.
The sable blackbird and the thrush
Do hold their council in the bush;
The chaffinch and the little wren
Set by the windy ways of men,
And where the gaping rocks are rent,
Convene their secret parliament.
So here, of harsher cares grown sick,
I sit my woolsack politic,
And think my country most doth gain
When I the inward law maintain:
For truest statesman sure is he
Who with the whole world doth agree,
Who seeks not either place or pelf,
Nor wills to govern but himself,
Who with the right of Right sufficed,
Discards all other wealth unprized.
And thus my happiness I find
Within the compass of my mind;
Forswearing all the good and ill
That answer not unto my will;

Nor fix the motion of my soul
In what lies out of my control,
Whilst in a nobler sphere I lean
To make my conscience pure and clean,
And more than mortal form do hold
The fitness of the spirit's mould.

No languid hours may here oppress
The soul's industrious idleness,
Whose lively forces still invent
Some new distraction to present,
And faithful energies protest
That wholesome labour lives with rest.
Thus when the sand of life is done
That doth our petty hopes outrun,
I fear not death, but hold in trust
The faith of honourable dust;
Nor let my courage sink dismayed
Because Time with my bones hath played,
Whose steadfast purpose linked with fate
Doth join Eternity its mate.

THE REST.

WHO hath no wish for rule, nor seeks for place,
    Or honour's grace;
But wills to be the master of his ways,
    Despising praise;
And though hot strife for gold rule all around,
Yet, still contented, keeps his sober bound;
    This man a rest shall have
Which those, though gaining their desire, shall crave.

When rich men point to fields and broad estates,
    He knows them baits
To care, and that for every crop is sown
    New cares are mown,
And troubles sickled with their autumn wheat:
So slippery is the tenure of the great;
    So short, so frail the zest
Of mortal pride and bravery at their best.

He firmly aims, within his constant mind,
    At truths behind
The painted shows of Time's deceptive things,
    Nor envies kings;

Ruling a realm within more vast and grand
Than titled acres of prolific land:
    His rich increase is more
Than all the wealth of their ingarnered store.

Whilst others passion serve and fierce desire,
    His tempered fire
Doth gently warm, and not consume, or dim
    The sun in him,
But adds a richer fragrance to the rose,
And every morn fresh gladness doth disclose,
    Flooding this earthly being
With those great lights that fill an angel's seeing.

Him every breeze that blows with airy voice
    Doth bid rejoice,
And every star that drowsy evening shows,
    To sleep compose;
Each bird that sings amongst the spreading trees
Is charged to him with heavenly messages,
    And blossoms breathe their smell
To scent the chambers where his soul doth dwell.

Stumble he may, but he can never fall,
    Or be the thrall
Of error; for through humbleness and love,
    His ways do prove

How in the path of pure simplicity
And singleness, the light of truth doth lie:
    Himself he sets aside,
In the great universal Law to bide.

And when at last he bids farewell to Time,
    He spreads, sublime,
Broad wings of faith and hope, and floats secure
    To haven sure,
And anchors where blue seas are always calm,
And every wind is fed with odoured balm;
    For faith doth hold him still
The steadfast pillar of his Maker's will.

SHEPHERD'S THRIFT.

I HOLD no ventures on the land,
    I send no ships upon the sea;
The winds that bear their wealth in hand,
    May blow which way they list for me:
My inward stores nor let me scant,
Nor pine for dearth when others want.

Content doth wall ambition's will,
    And tame the fury of those fires,
Whose flames do strive to overfill
    The level of my low desires:
The fierce delirium of the great
Doth never tempt my humble state.

No wind of praise my mind doth move,
    No breath of blame my course may swerve;
Sufficient for my own behove,
    Myself unto myself I serve:
I have, I hold, I hope, I trust,
Nor take my measure from the dust.

My faith is firm: no coward fears
    Do shake the triumph of my soul,
Swept on the wings of circling spheres
    That round the vast empyrean roll,
Content, when Time my pulse hath stilled,
A Destiny should be fulfilled.

Whilst laurelled victors conquering go,
    And stretch their rule from land to land,
Nor heed what vast mutations flow
    To wrest the sceptre from their hand,
Lord of myself, whate'er betide,
I reign and rule the world beside.

No lark doth lift the brow of morn,
    No eagle kiss the flaming sun,
But straight my ravished soul is borne
    Along the paths where they do run :
Such high-topt glories I do find
In airy regions of the mind.

I lean upon the orient bands
    That bind the circuit of the day ;
I feel the touch of angel hands
    That lead me from the earth away ;

I dwell on shores more rich with gold
Than feigned Pactolus ever roll'd.

Herein my heart is bound and fixed,
    Unto this law I most incline;
The Power these elements hath mixed,
    May bid recall them to the mine;
But I shall rise when they decay,
To empire of a mightier sway.

THE SHEPHERD'S GOOD NIGHT.

OH, blessed Night, who dost from care assoil
    The careful soul, and bid revive again
Those tender voices in the press and moil
    Of travailed day concealed and hushed had lain,
Thou bringest rest unto the poor man's toil,
    And pourest balm upon the sick man's pain ;
Thou takest all the world within thine arms,
Soothing its troubled breathings by thy charms.

Wrapt in thy filmy stole of dusky grey,
    Thou hidest us from grief and lean despair,
And rolling all these earthly clouds away,
    Dost ope the gate of that celestial stair
Whereon white angels tread, whose brows display
    Immortal garlands through their golden hair,
Who bringing smiles and whispers soft and light,
Watch by lone couches through the livelong night.

Touched by thy hand the crimson blushing rose,
    Drawing its petaled curtains, falls asleep ;
In wattled pens the folded flocks repose,
    Whilst winds are hushed and moon and stars do peep ;

The new-made mother clasps her babe more close,
   Dear babes more closely to their mothers creep;
Such melting thoughts are born from thy soft kiss
As steep sweet lovers in deep dreams of bliss.

Now bats and moths and owls begin to stir,
   And swarthy night-elves trip it on the grass,
And fairies, liveried in gossamer,
   With twining hands and twinkling footsteps pass;
Soft whispers fall from slumbering birch and fir;
   Each rustic shepherd hies him to his lass;
The weary hours are washed in silvery dews;
Such grace thou dost through all the world diffuse.

Now doth sweet Philomel in loud complaint,
   Make all the woodland chambers ring and thrill
With the sad story which she first did paint
   In woven lines, of cruel Tereus' ill,
Then with her heavy passion sick and faint,
   She leans against a thorn and fain would still
Her anguished sorrows on the spine it wears;
For this she finds less sharp than those she bears.

The seaman on the crystal-bosomed deep,
   Trims his white sail and turns his prow tow'rds home,

Whereas his faithful spouse high watch doth keep
    Beneath the azure of heav'n's spangled dome,
Asking no boon of weary-lidded sleep
    Until her much-expected lord shall come.
Lo, yonder beacon from the window burn
With steady light invites his swift return.

O golden star of happy Human Love
    Lit by the splendid fires of Love Divine,
Though envious clouds day's sunshine may remove,
    No depth of cloud shall ever darken thine;
For thy supernal radiance high above
    These misty vapours holds empyreal line;
Thou dost dispose all mortal things to even,
Soothed into peace by harmonies of heaven!—

Lord of the Night, great King and God of Day,
    Whom all men worship under several names,
Thou who dost all this wondrous world upstay,
    Clothed in the tempest, crowned with shining flames,
Whose power the raging winds and seas obey,
    Whose hand the painted flower to beauty frames,
Who holdest all thy creatures in thine eye,
God of high grace, of might and majesty:

Let beams go forth of Thee as day and night
    Bring in their round of toil and wholesome rest,

And in the glory of a better light,
    Men's hearts be fed and nourished on the best,
Enlarge thy people with the broader sight
    To see that all the world by Thee is blest,
And Death and Life are but the ministers
Of those vast ends thy wider purpose stirs.

For what is man : what are we but the leaves
    That hang upon thy wide-dispreading tree,
Whose veinèd branching world with world enweaves,
    And makes the universe a part of Thee ?
What though we fall : what though these Time-fed
    sheaves
    To nobler purpose destined, garnered be !
Enough that Thou the Lord remain the same,
Though we, thy creatures, change each day our name.

We change and fly as mist before the sun ;
    Our life a fleeting day-time doth present ;
We love and hate, and then our glass is run,
    And all the talents gone which Thou hast lent ;
Our term decay : our course is scarce begun
    Ere we do find our portioned measure spent.
Be Thou our anchor, and our haven be,
Whose sober trust and hope are staid on Thee.

Bring down thy heavens in glory to the earth,
    Or let the earth ascend to where Thou art;
Awake within us those pure springs whose birth
    First found a flowing in the Master's heart;
Let clasping hands and trust and honest worth
    Bind every human creature each a part
Of one united being growing still
From good to good into thy Perfect Will.

THE END.

By the same Author, Crown 8vo., price 6s., cloth.

SONGS OF A WAYFARER.

OPINIONS OF THE PRESS.

"Had Mr. Davies' poems been published two hundred years ago, the world would now be quoting them as marvellous examples of poetic grace and sentiment."—*Examiner.*

"Passing from the author's faults to his merits, we feel a pleasure in inviting special attention to a poem called 'The Garden,' which, from its calm and classical sweetness, would appear to be modelled after Ben Jonson, or some of his followers, and which, in its own particular style, appears to us to be almost perfect. We should willingly give an extract from this little gem, if we could legitimately do so; but it would be like cutting a single figure from an historical group, or treating the works of a landscape-painter like an Ordnance map."—*Athenæum.*

"The 'Wayfarer' must doubtless take his place among the poets of our day."—*London Quarterly Review.*

"It is not often that an unknown writer, coming before us with an unheralded volume of verse, claims a kindlier recognition than is due to Mr. Davies for the present book."—*Pall Mall Gazette.*

"These songs flow from a mind that contains as genuine a vein of poetry as has been revealed for some time. . . . We feel that, in noticing a volume of this kind, specimens, not descriptions, are wanted; and yet there is difficulty in knowing what to quote, the songs are so uniformly excellent. Yet to describe one peculiarity a trial must be made. That sense of indefiniteness—that feeling as if the poet had not said everything, but left you much to create—that condensation carried to such a pitch that the reader, feeling within him emotions not manifestly called up by the lines which he has read, fancies that he owes them to himself—all this is present."—*Scotsman.*

"Mr. Davies writes like a modernized Herrick: modernized, it must be understood, both in language and thought, for there is nothing of the grossness that disfigures the 'Hesperides.'"—*Spectator.*

"'Songs of a Wayfarer' are the product of a highly-cultured mind and a genuinely poetic temperament."—*Daily Telegraph.*

"We not only offer Mr. Davies a hearty welcome to the realms of poesy, but predict for him a warm reception and a lasting place in popular esteem."—*Illustrated Times.*

Also by the same Author, just published, with Woodcuts and a Map, 8vo., cloth extra, price 18s.

THE PILGRIMAGE OF THE TIBER,
FROM ITS MOUTH TO ITS SOURCE;
With some Account of its Tributaries.

OPINIONS OF THE PRESS.

"This is a charming book from beginning to end. . . . We end as we began, by commending the book most heartily to our readers."—*Athenæum.*

"This is a pleasant book by a cultivated man, and a substantial addition to the library of the traveller in Italy, whom it will lead to spots of rare beauty and interest undreamt of by the conventional crowd of tourists, and hitherto but slenderly referred to by the best guide-books."—*Spectator.*

"A very charming book . . . admirably illustrated. We can recommend the book most heartily."—*Standard.*

"We can pay Mr. Davies no higher compliment, and we can bestow upon his work no greater commendation, than when we say he has succeeded in making the interest of his 'Pilgrimage' co-extensive with that of his theme. . . . While we tender our thanks to the author we should not forget the artist. The illustrations which accompany the letterpress are as faithful as they are choice."—*Conservative.*

"The author tells his tale so well that we gladly welcome it as a pleasant addition to the number of books of Italian travel."—*Tablet.*

"We have found it difficult, or rather impossible, to give our readers, in the allotted space, any adequate idea of the beauties of this delightful volume. It is a book for the learned, for the poet, for the historian, for the lover of legendary lore, for the artist and for the general reader. Moreover, it is most exquisitely written, a fine and finished piece of modern literature. The engravings, copied from drawings or sketches taken on the spot, are most successfully executed, and add much to the charm of the text."—*Literary World.*

www.ingramcontent.com/pod-product-compliance
Lightning Source LLC
Chambersburg PA
CBHW030305170426
43202CB00009B/877